KEYBOARD PERCUSSION

FILM FAVORITES

Solos and Band Arrangements
Correlated with Essential Elements® Band Method

Arranged by
MICHAEL SWEENEY, JOHN MOSS and PAUL LAVENDER

Welcome to ESSENTIAL ELEMENTS FILM FAVORITES! The arrangements in this versatile book can be used either in a full concert band setting or as solos for individual instruments. The SOLO pages appear at the beginning of the book, followed by the BAND ARRANGEMENT pages. The supplemental CD recording or PIANO ACCOMPANIMENT book may be used as an accompaniment for solo performance.

ISBN 978-0-634-08706-6

HAL•LEONARD®
CORPORATION
7777 W. BLUEMOUND RD. P.O. BOX 13819 MILWAUKEE, WI 53213

00860156

PIRATES OF THE CARIBBEAN

(A medley including: The Medallion Calls • The Black Pearl)

KEYBOARD PERCUSSION
Solo

Music by **KLAUS BADELT**
Arranged by **MICHAEL SWEENEY**

From the Paramount and Twentieth Century Fox Motion Picture TITANIC

MY HEART WILL GO ON

(Love Theme From 'Titanic')

KEYBOARD PERCUSSION
Solo

Music by JAMES HORNER
Lyric by WILL JENNINGS
Arranged by JOHN MOSS

THE RAINBOW CONNECTION

KEYBOARD PERCUSSION
Solo

Words and Music by
PAUL WILLIAMS and **KENNETH L. ASCHER**
Arranged by PAUL LAVENDER

Easy Three

From THE LORD OF THE RINGS: THE FELLOWSHIP OF THE RING

MAY IT BE

KEYBOARD PERCUSSION
Solo

**Words and Music by EITHNE NI BHRAONAIN,
NICKY RYAN and ROMA RYAN**
Arranged by JOHN MOSS

00860156

From Walt Disney Pictures' TARZAN™

YOU'LL BE IN MY HEART

KEYBOARD PERCUSSION
Solo

Words and Music by
PHIL COLLINS
Arranged by MICHAEL SWEENEY

From the Motion Picture SHREK 2

ACCIDENTALLY IN LOVE

KEYBOARD PERCUSSION
Solo

**Words and Music by
ADAM F. DURITZ**
Arranged by MICHAEL SWEENEY

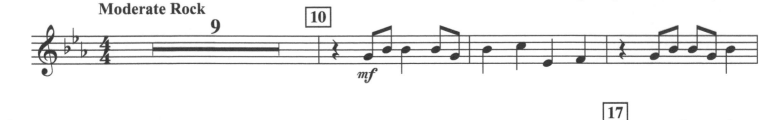

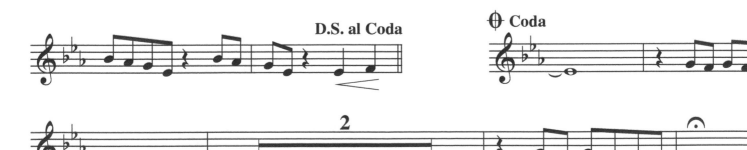

ALSO SPRACH ZARATHUSTRA

KEYBOARD PERCUSSION
Solo

By Richard Strauss
Arranged by MICHAEL SWEENEY

From the Paramount Motion Picture MISSION: IMPOSSIBLE

MISSION: IMPOSSIBLE THEME

KEYBOARD PERCUSSION
Solo

By LALO SCHIFRIN
Arranged by MICHAEL SWEENEY

From SHREK

MUSIC FROM SHREK

(A medley including: Fairytale Opening • Ride The Dragon)

KEYBOARD PERCUSSION
Solo

Music by JOHN POWELL
and HARRY GREGSON-WILLIAMS
Arranged by JOHN MOSS

00860156

From the TriStar Motion Picture THE MASK OF ZORRO

ZORRO'S THEME

KEYBOARD PERCUSSION
Solo

Composed by
JAMES HORNER
Arranged by JOHN MOSS

Heroically

00860156

PIRATES OF THE CARIBBEAN

(A medley including: The Medallion Calls • The Black Pearl)

KEYBOARD PERCUSSION
Band Arrangement

Music by KLAUS BADELT
Arranged by MICHAEL SWEENEY

"The Medallion Calls"
Majestically

Optional Faster Tempo

"The Black Pearl"

From the Paramount and Twentieth Century Fox Motion Picture TITANIC

MY HEART WILL GO ON

(Love Theme From 'Titanic')

KEYBOARD PERCUSSION
Band Arrangement

Music by JAMES HORNER
Lyric by WILL JENNINGS
Arranged by JOHN MOSS

From THE MUPPET MOVIE
THE RAINBOW CONNECTION

KEYBOARD PERCUSSION
Band Arrangement

Words and Music by
PAUL WILLIAMS and KENNETH L. ASCHER
Arranged by PAUL LAVENDER

00860156

From THE LORD OF THE RINGS: THE FELLOWSHIP OF THE RING
MAY IT BE

KEYBOARD PERCUSSION
Band Arrangement

**Words and Music by EITHNE NI BHRAONAIN,
NICKY RYAN and ROMA RYAN**
Arranged by JOHN MOSS

From Walt Disney Pictures' TARZAN™

YOU'LL BE IN MY HEART

KEYBOARD PRECUSSION
Band Arrangement

Words and Music by
PHIL COLLINS
Arranged by MICHAEL SWEENEY

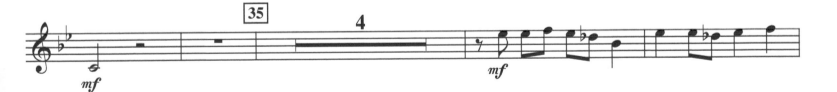

00860156

From the Motion Picture SHREK 2
ACCIDENTALLY IN LOVE

KEYBOARD PERCUSSION
Band Arrangement

Words and Music by
ADAM F. DURITZ
Arranged by MICHAEL SWEENEY

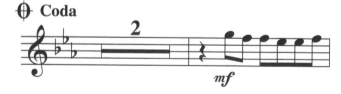

00860156

Featured in the Motion Picture 2001: A SPACE ODYSSEY

ALSO SPRACH ZARATHUSTRA

KEYBOARD PERCUSSION
Band Arrangement

By RICHARD STRAUSS
Arranged by MICHAEL SWEENEY

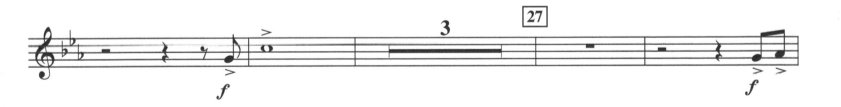

From the Paramount Motion Picture MISSION: IMPOSSIBLE

MISSION: IMPOSSIBLE THEME

KEYBOARD PERCUSSION
Band Arrangement

By LALO SCHIFRIN
Arranged by MICHAEL SWEENEY

From SHREK

MUSIC FROM SHREK

(A medley including: Fairytale Opening • Ride The Dragon)

KEYBOARD PERCUSSION
Band Arrangement

Music by JOHN POWELL and HARRY GREGSON-WILLIAMS
Arranged by JOHN MOSS

00860156

From the TriStar Motion Picture THE MASK OF ZORRO

ZORRO'S THEME

KEYBOARD PERCUSSION
Band Arrangement

Composed by JAMES HORNER
Arranged by JOHN MOSS

Heroically